Doggie Data

Beagles

MARGARET MINCKS

BLACK RABBIT BOOKS

Bolt is published by Black Rabbit Books
P.O. Box 227, Mankato, Minnesota, 56002.
www.blackrabbitbooks.com

Jennifer Besel, editor; Grant Gould, interior designer; Michael Sellner, cover designer; Omay Ayres, photo researcher

Library of Congress Cataloging-in-Publication Data
Names: Mincks, Margaret, author.
Title: Beagles / by Margaret Mincks.
Description: Mankato, Minnesota : Black Rabbit Books, [2018] | Series: Bolt. Doggie data | Audience: Ages 9-12. | Audience: Grades 4 to 6. | Includes bibliographical references and index.
Identifiers: LCCN 2016049954 (print) | LCCN 2017003481 (ebook) | ISBN 9781680721485 (library binding) | ISBN 9781680722123 (e-book) | ISBN 9781680724516 (paperback)
Subjects: LCSH: Beagle (Dog breed)–Juvenile literature.
Classification: LCC SF429.B3 M56 2018 (print) | LCC SF429.B3 (ebook) | DDC 636.753/7-dc23
LC record available at https://lccn.loc.gov/2016049954

Printed in the United States at CG Book Printers, North Mankato, Minnesota, 56003. 3/17

Image Credits

123RF: lunja, 4–5; Alamy: CPC Collection, 27 (bottom); GROSSEMY VANESSA, 24 (bloodhound); Stephen Flint, 13; iStock: AleksandarNakic, 7; Memitina, 3; Solovyova, 10; Shutterstock: anetapics, 20–21 (puppy); Annette Shaff, 16–17; Buffy1982, 20–21 (senior); Easy Morning, 14–15; Ekachai Stocker, 19; Eric Isselee, 10–11 (infographic dogs); Erik Lam, 28; Ermolaev Alexander, 23 (bottom two); Everita Pane, 32; Halfpoint, 6–7; Igor Normann, 20–21 (adolescent); Kateryna Mostova, 24 (beagle); kukuruxa, 25 (Yorkshire); Lesley Rigg, 31; markos86, 8–9; martinho Smart, 23 (bath); Napat, Cover; Ross Stevenson, 1, 27, Back Cover; Samuel Lam, 21 (adult); Solov-iova Liudmyla, 14; Svetography, 24 (cocker spaniel); tsik, 18; Vivienstock, 25 (beagle)
Every effort has been made to contact copyright holders for material reproduced in this book. Any omissions will be rectified in subsequent printings if notice is given to the publisher.

Contents

CHAPTER 1

Meet the Beagle

The small beagle races after the ball. Its ears flop in the wind. The dog skids to a stop as it comes to the ball. Then it races back to its owner.

Suddenly, the dog sniffs the air. It has caught the smell of something interesting. The beagle doesn't want to play ball anymore. It follows its nose to find out what the smell is.

A Happy, Hungry Hound

Beagles are small, friendly dogs. They love to hunt, play, howl, and eat. Beagles belong to a group called the scent hounds. Scent hounds use their noses to learn about the world. Beagles follow their noses everywhere.

How Big Is a Beagle?

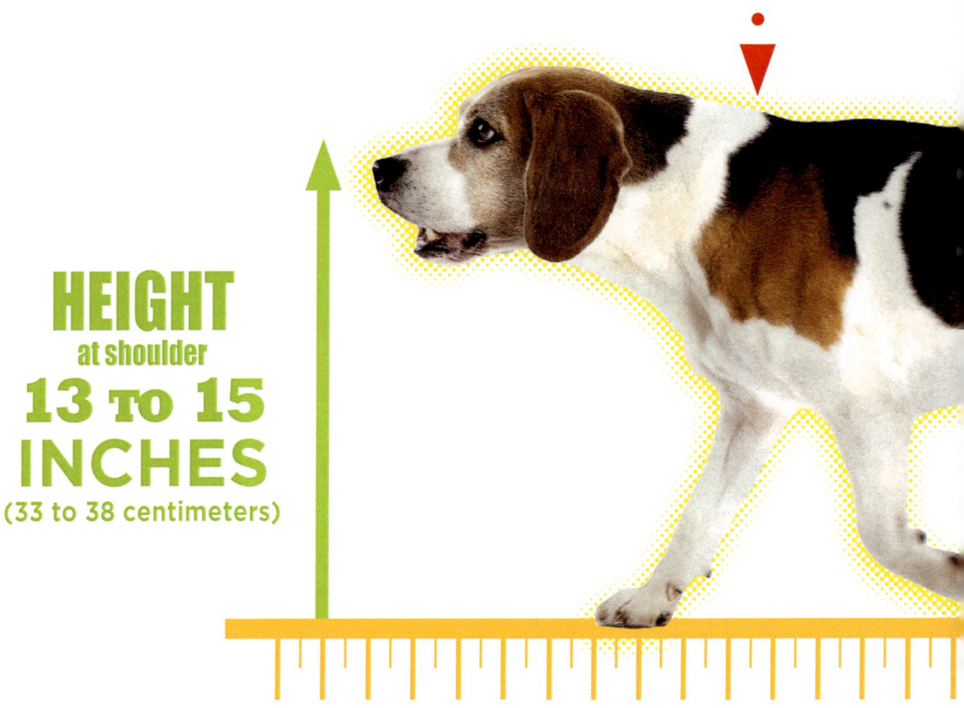

0
pounds
5
10
15
20
25
30
35
40
45
50
pounds
WEIGHT
18 TO 30
POUNDS
(8 to 14 kilograms)

PARTS OF A BEAGLE

LARGE BROWN EYES
SQUARE MUZZLE
SHORT-HAIRED COAT

TOP 10 MOST POPULAR Dogs in the United States in 2015

1 Labrador Retrievers

2 German Shepherds

3 Golden Retrievers

4 Bulldogs

CHAPTER 2

A Special Personality

Many people love beagles. These dogs are friendly. They also play nicely with kids and other pets.

Noisy and Stubborn

Beagles make a lot of noise. They are known for howling. Sometimes beagles howl when they're hungry. They will also bark when they're bored or lonely. Beagles' loud voices make them good watchdogs. But owners might have trouble keeping their dogs quiet.

Beagles can be stubborn too. Training them requires patience. Most beagles would rather follow a scent than a **command**.

Beagles make three different kinds of sounds. They bark, howl, and bay.

CHAPTER 3

Beagles' Features

Beagles are small, **sturdy** dogs. Most don't weigh more than 30 pounds (14 kg).

Beagles come in many colors. The most common combination is called tricolor. Tricolor dogs are black, white, and tan. Beagles can also be red, yellow, brown, and gray.

Smelling Food

Beagles have an excellent sense of smell. They are always sniffing for food. If a beagle smells food, it will run off to find it.

Some people call beagles "chowhounds." These dogs always seem hungry. Beagles may even steal food from their owners!

Scent Receptors in Humans and Dogs

300 million
225 million
225 million
125 million
100 million
150 million
200 million
250 million
300 million

Beagles live for about 12 to 15 years.

Beagle Health Problems

Beagles love to eat. If they eat too much, they will become overweight. Too much weight causes back problems and **joint** issues.

Sometimes beagles' eyelid **glands** swell and turn red. This problem is called cherry eye.

Beagle Life Cycle

Beagles are almost 80 percent of their adult size by six months old.

PUPPY

Beagles become seniors at around eight years old. Senior beagles move more slowly.

SENIOR

ADOLESCENT

ADULT

By nine months old, beagles are almost fully grown. They still act like puppies, though!

Beagles are fully grown by their second birthdays.

CHAPTER 4

Caring for Beagles

All dogs need regular vet checkups. They also need care at home. Beagles' coats need weekly brushing. They only need a few baths each year. Nails should be trimmed monthly. Their teeth need brushing a few times a week.

Beagles' ears need special attention. Their hanging ears can get infections easily. Owners have to clean beagles' ears carefully.

Beagle Grooming

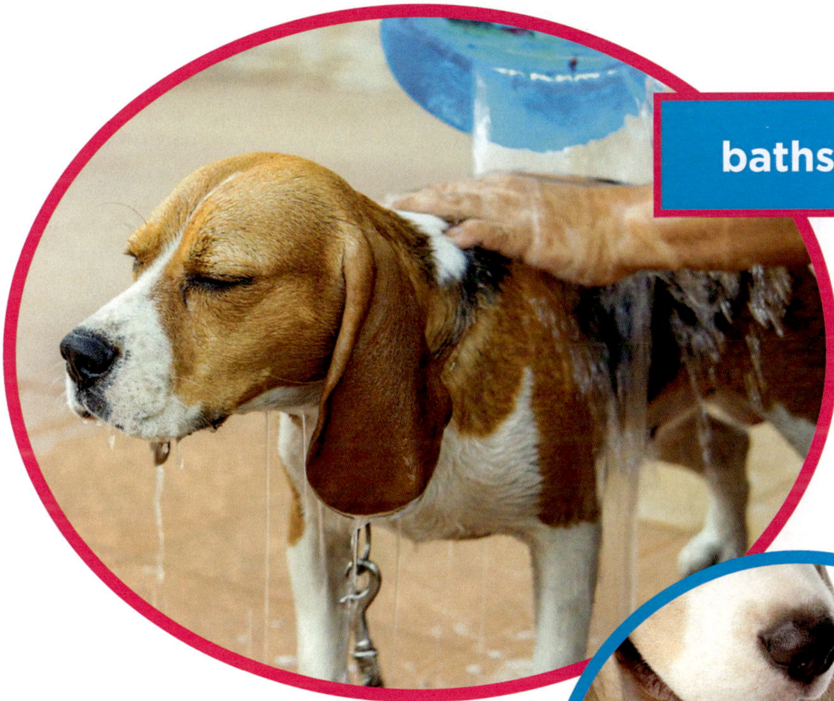

baths

nail trimming

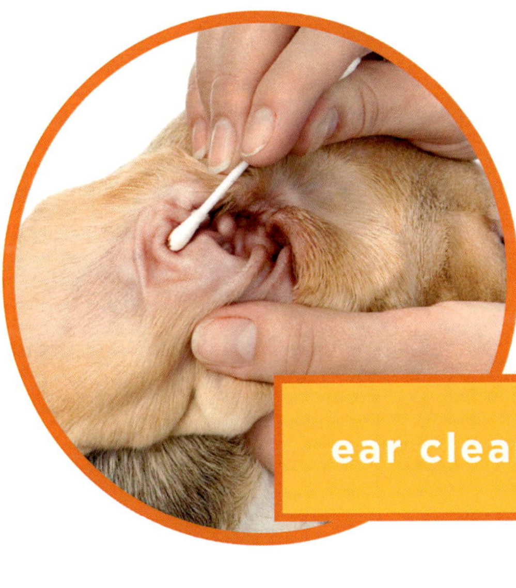

ear cleaning

COMPARING SIZES
BLOODHOUND
COCKER SPANIEL
80 to 110 POUNDS (36 to 50 kg)
20 to 30 POUNDS (9 to 14 kg)

Eating and Exercising

Many beagles eat twice a day. Veterinarians help owners decide how much food dogs should eat. Beagles are always hungry. They might beg for more, even if they've had enough.

These dogs need daily walks and regular playtime. Experts say beagles should get one hour of exercise a day. Keep beagles on leashes during walks. Otherwise their curious noses could lead them away.

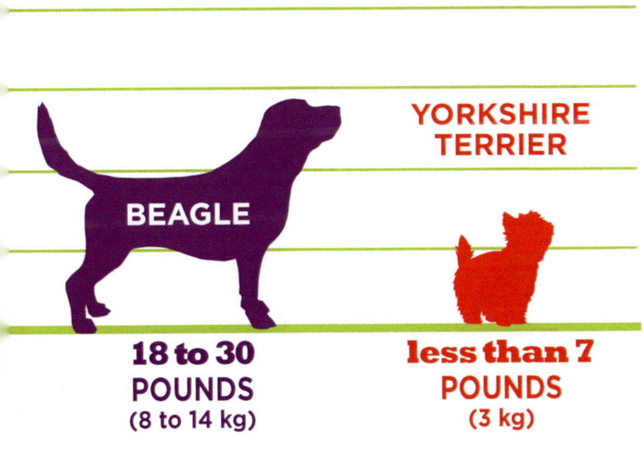

A Friendly, Howling Thief

Beagles' happy, friendly attitudes make them popular dogs. These hounds have big personalities and even bigger voices. They might steal your food. But they'll also steal your heart.

A group of dogs called the Beagle Brigade works at airports. The dogs sniff packages for airport security.

Is a Beagle Right for You?

Answer the questions below. Then add up your points to see if a beagle is a good fit.

1 What do you do when a dog howls or barks?

A. I laugh. Dogs will be dogs! (3 points)

B. I hope it quiets down soon. (2 points)

C. I cover my ears and groan. (1 point)

2 Do you like when a dog follows you everywhere?

A. No. I like an independent dog. (3 points)

B. I like attention, but I also like my space. (2 points)

C. Yes! I always want my dog by my side! (1 point)

3 Do you like taking your dog out for exercise?

A. Yes! It's fun for both of us. (3 points)

B. Sometimes. (2 points)

C. I'd rather stay inside. (1 point)

3 points
A beagle is not your perfect match.

4–8 points
You could be a beagle's friend. But there might be a better breed for you.

9 points
You're totally ready to be a beagle's buddy!

GLOSSARY

adolescent (ad-oh-LES-uhnt)—a young person or animal that is developing into an adult

bay (BAY)—to bark with long sounds

command (kuh-MAND)—an order given to a person or animal to do something

gland (GLAND)—a body part that produces a substance to be used by the body or given off from it

joint (JOYNT)—a point where two bones meet in the body

muzzle (MUH-zuhl)—the usually long nose and mouth of an animal

receptor (ree-SEP-tuhr)—a nerve ending that senses changes in light, temperature, pressure, or other things and causes the body to react to it

sturdy (STUR-dee)—strong and healthy

BOOKS

Bodden, Valerie. *Beagles.* Fetch! Mankato, MN: Creative Education, 2014.

Johnson, Jinny. *Beagle.* My Favorite Dog. Mankato, MN: Smart Apple Media, 2013.

Schuh, Mari. *Beagles.* Awesome Dogs. Minneapolis: Bellwether Media, 2016.

WEBSITES

Beagle Dog Breed Information
www.akc.org/dog-breeds/beagle/

Beagle Guide
www.animalplanet.com/breed-selector/dog-breeds/hound/beagle.html

Pets: Taking Care of Your Pet
pbskids.org/itsmylife/family/pets/article7.html

INDEX